Palm-reading is not just for Gypsies! Everyone has the ability to understand his or her present and future by simply looking at the palm. Each one of us is born with lines, signs and mounds on our palm. Now, with this easy-to-use guide, you can find out about yourself and those around you. The answers are in the palm of your hand! The Little Big Book includes illustrations to help you to understand how to read your palm and how to apply palmistry to your everyday life.

Batia Shorek has been a professional palm-reader for many years. She offers courses and gives lectures on various mystical subjects, and has been published in professional journals. This is her second book on palmistry. She lives in Israel with her husband and two children.

LITTLE **BIG** BOOK

SERIES:

LITTLE **BIG** BOOK

of

Basic Palmistry

by Batia Shorek

Astrolog Publishing House

Astrolog Publishing House
P.O. Box 1123, Hod Hasharon 45111, Israel
Tel./Fax: 972-9-7412044
E-Mail: info@astrolog.co.il
Astrolog Web Site: www.astrolog.co.il

© Batia Shorek 1998

ISBN 965-494-043-4

Published by Astrolog Publishing House 1998

Distribution:
U.S.A. & CANADA by APG -
Associated Publishers Group
U.K. & EUROPE by DEEP BOOKS
EAST ASIA by CKK Ltd.

Printed in Israel
10 9 8 7 6 5 4 3 2 1

WHY THE PALM?

The linguistic definition of the hand is really quite simple: it is the part of the human body found at the end of the arm, and is used for holding and touching things. But the hand is really so much more than that. It is the part of our body through which we come in contact with the material world. The hands are not just another pair of extremities that cannot be used for walking. The ability to grasp objects, thanks to the structure of the opposing thumb, makes our hands become much more important than merely another pair of appendages.

There are philosophers who claim that the development of the human palm is, in essence, the development of civilization. Prehistoric man, resembling the monkey, could hold only stones and branches in his hand. Over time, numerous tools and devices were developed for use by man's hands. And if we compare the palm of the hand with the sole of the foot, we immediately see how appropriate - or inappropriate - the tools and devices with which we come into daily contact are to the palm of the hand.

Of all the parts of the hand, it is the thumb

which stands out in importance. The muscular flexibility of the thumb and its unique opposable structure vis-a`-vis the other fingers are what differentiate, according to some, between man and ape (anatomically speaking).

The hand is important not only as an anatomical expression of man, but also as a psychological expression. There are nervous hands, sensitive hands, lazy hands and "lefties". We often endow hands with characteristic traits. No one speaks of lazy thighs or nervous ears, but a person's hands reflect his character, and therefore they reflect the same characteristics and talents as the person to whom they belong.

One of the most interesting things about the hand is skin responsiveness. The skin at the tip of the fingers, for example, is quite sensitive (second in sensitivity only to the skin on the lips). The palm is more sensitive than the back of the hand, while the underside of the fingers is quite tough. Sensitivity is determined by the number of nerve endings found beneath the surface of the skin. The way in which the nerve endings are distributed in the palm of the hand is both anatomically and psychologically significant.

The hand is a sophisticated tool for

touching and feeling, and its sensitivity can sometimes reach incredible levels, such as with the hands of a blind person or other people whose sense of touch is more developed than their other senses.

The lines on the palm are constantly changing, but they are all influenced by similar rules. The structure of the Life Line, for example, is influenced by muscular changes at the base of the thumb; the Heart Line is affected by the muscles which close the palm; the Head Line is influenced by the contrast between the hand and the fingers, and so on. The fact that these lines get their shape from and can be changed by the muscles as they react to a person's activities, needs and impulses is what gives these lines their significance.

The surface of the skin is like a sensitive record which absorbs and retains a person's needs and impulses, and reveals them to the palmist who possesses the knowledge to interpret what is written there. Therefore, despite various attempts at reading a person's character using other parts of the body, it is palmistry that has been most successful and has gained the most followers.

CHIROGNOMY

Chirognomy and Chiromancy

Palmistry can really be divided into two main branches:

Chirognomy - the branch of palmistry dealing with the shape of the hand and the fingers.

Chiromancy - the branch of palmistry dealing with the lines and mounts found on the palm.

THE SIZE OF THE HAND

Examine the palm relative to the size of the body, and primarily, relative to the size of the arm.

Relatively large hands indicate a person who likes to take care of details and possesses an ability to perform delicate and complex work.

Relatively small hands belong to people who have great ideas; they indicate intuition and quick thinking, but also signify a lack of care and a tendency to exaggerate their own abilities.

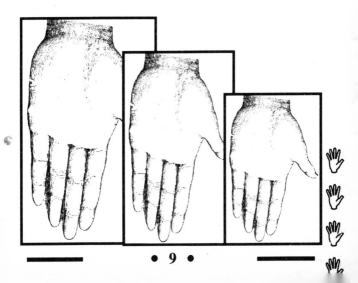

THE SKIN AND FEEL
OF THE PALM

These two characteristics are examined by feeling and pressing on the palm.

A thin palm with dry skin indicates a person who is nervous and bashful.

A thick palm signifies sensuality.

A weak palm indicates a hesitant and lazy character.

A stable, flexible palm shows a person with intelligence and moderation.

A great deal of experience is required in order to able to identify the character of the person's palm with the first touch.

THE FINGERS

The fingers should be examined with regard to their shape, length, relation to each other, and so forth. For the novice, it is sufficient to look at the joints of the fingers and the relationship between the joint and the phalanx, or bone between the joints of the fingers, in order to classify the characteristics of the fingers.

Prominent finger joints indicate an ability to analyze and concentrate, and often, a talent for science and mathematics.

Very smooth finger joints tell us about intuition, impulsiveness and artistic abilities.

THE THUMB

Without first examining the thumb, it will be impossible to gain a truly deep understanding of the person's palm. The special characteristics of the thumb differentiate between man and the chimpanzee, for example. The thumb is particularly important in analyzing a person's palm. It represents essential strengths and indicates the energy level in a person's nature.

A relatively long thumb indicates intellectual prowess, sensitivity, and a strong character.

A short thumb usually signifies a nature that is controlled by material pleasures.

A short, slender thumb shows an inability to make decisions and persevere.

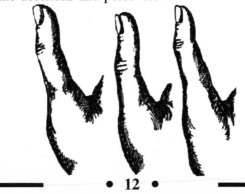

THE FIRST PHALANX OF THE THUMB

The phalanx with the fingernail is most important in analyzing the palm, because at the same time we examine the nails, from which we can learn much regarding the person's character. The first phalanx represents a person's will, generally speaking.

When this phalanx is well-developed, it indicates a strong and developed personality.

If it is narrow and pointed at the end, it signifies that the person's energies are being wasted or are not being utilized.

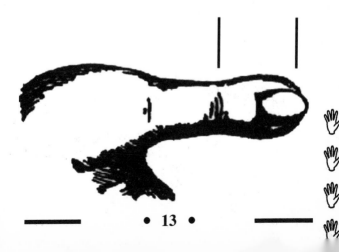

THE SECOND PHALANX
OF THE THUMB

This phalanx is linked to an individual's logic and represents his tendency to compromise. It should be about the same length as the first phalanx, indicating intelligence, imagination, and moderation.

If it is thicker than the first phalanx, it shows self-discipline, stubbornness and a tendency to be overly cautious.

If it is thinner than the first phalanx, it is a sign of indecisiveness and emotionalism.

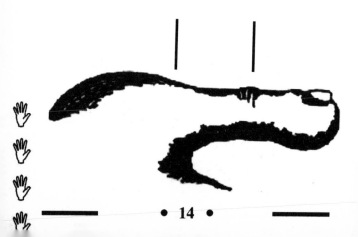

THE FINGERS

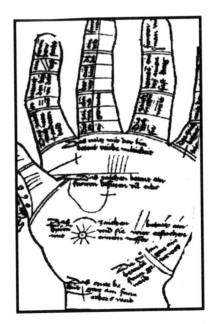

THE INDEX FINGER
(next to the thumb, the "pointer")

It is particularly important to analyze this finger because it "places the thumb a proper distance from the rest of the fingers", as the famous Chiro himself claimed.

The first finger is sometimes referred to as the finger of Jupiter, and reflects ambition and pride.

When this finger is long, it signifies a desire to succeed. When it is especially long (that is, as long as the middle finger), it indicates a strong desire for power.

If the index finger is short, it signifies a great deal of sensitivity, an artistic nature and a tendency towards solitude.

If the finger is straight, it indicates a great ability for study.

If it is bent towards the middle finger, it is a sign of a person who is introverted and a loner.

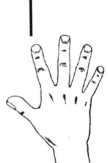

THE MIDDLE FINGER

This finger is controlled by Saturn, and represents one's personality.

An elongated finger indicates over-intellectuality and difficulty in adapting to new people and situations.

A thick, prominent finger signifies a person who is calculating and serious.

If the finger is particularly broad in relation to the other fingers, it means that the person is pessimistic, with a tendency toward depression and illness.

A short middle finger indicates impulsiveness, intuition and imagination.

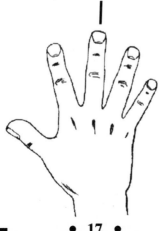

THE RING FINGER
(next to the pinkie)

Traditionally, analyzing this finger is particularly important in women.

This finger is referred to as the finger of Apollo, and is related to the emotions.

A finger of average length indicates a person who is psychologically balanced.

An elongated finger means intelligence and emotional enlightenment.

A short finger shows emotional problems and difficulties in adapting to other people and the demands of the world at large.

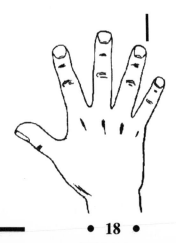

THE PINKIE

On the other side of the hand, farthest from the thumb, is the pinkie, which serves to a great extent as a balance for the thumb.

This is the finger of Mercury, and it relates to a person's relationships with others.

If the pinkie is located further from the ring finger, it indicates difficulties in forming emotional relationships and expressing real thoughts and emotions.

If the first phalanx of the pinkie is long, this means good linguistic control.

It the finger is somewhat bent, this may indicate a certain amount of unfairness.

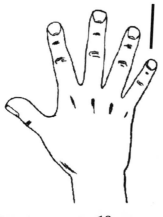

THE LENGTH
OF THE FINGERS

The length of the fingers is measured against the size of the palm. The problem is that the fingers are usually of different sizes, and it takes a great deal of skill to analyze the properties of each and every finger in relation to its size.

Fingers are considered to be long when the length of the middle finger is equal to the length of the palm.

A middle finger longer than the length of the palm is quite rare.

In general, long fingers (relative to the palm) indicate a well-developed intellect, while relatively short fingers indicate being in control of one's emotions.

SHAPES OF THE HAND

Palms are divided into several types: Various schools talk about four, five, seven or even nine types of hand shapes. In this book we will discuss the division accepted by most palmists.

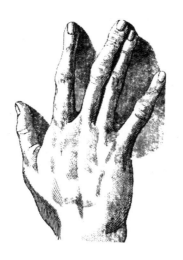

THE BASIC (ELEMENTAL) HAND

The shape of this hand is thick and broad, with few lines. The thumb, fingers and nails are short and wide. People with this type of hand lack intellect and a well-developed imagination; they are not interested in the arts. These are earth-bound people, slow and cautious. They have strong bodies and usually enjoy good health. But they require a great deal of rest; when they are fatigued, they can become angry quickly. If they become ill, their recovery is slow and they refuse to follow the advice of their physicians. They are conservative, enjoy familiar and safe surroun-dings, and are contemptuous of new ideas and innovations. They are materialistic people. Wealth and magnitude impress them.

They are sensuous and emotional, and are strongly attracted to members of the opposite sex. They are hot-blooded, stubborn and act instinctively. Some palmists call this type of hand "the laborer's hand".

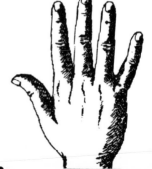

THE PRACTICAL HAND

The practical hand is square in shape. The length of the palm is equal to the width, and the nails are also short and square-shaped. A person with this type of hand is thought to be practical, methodical, independent and honest. He respects authority, discipline, strength and order. He is generally conservative in his opinions, although he is not narrow-minded.

People with this type of hand tend to be stubborn, resolute and strong-willed. They are particularly successful as politicians, business people, lawyers, teachers and scientists, but not in professions that require a creative, artistic strength.

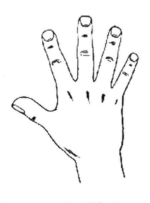

THE SPATULATE HAND

This type of hand is broader near the base of the fingers. The fingers are also broad and flat at the ends. People with this type of hand tend to be sly, ambitious, independent, and energetic. They pursue their goals stubbornly, and they often succeed in accumulating great wealth and power. They are able to overcome their failures and disappointments successfully.

These are intelligent people, original thinkers, and are most successful as scientists, inventors, engineers and artists.

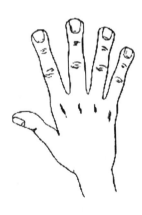

THE PHILOSOPHICAL HAND

This type of hand is long; the fingers are extended, with prominent joints and squared-off tips. People with this hand are particularly intelligent, with a well-developed imagination and good intuition.

People with this type of hand have been gifted with extrasensory perception (ESP), primarily telepathy (mind reading) and an ability to predict the future. They are individualistic and spiritually developed, and they like to analyze and judge situations and people. They generally tend not to reveal their emotions and thoughts, and they astound more conservative people with their original ideas.

They sometimes dress unconventionally in order to express their opposition to the ordinary. Many of them are successful in the arts, teaching, science and medicine, and have gained fame and recognition. People of this type do not make friends easily, but they can foster long-term friendships on an intellectual and emotional basis.

THE CONICAL HAND

This type of hand is also referred to as the artistic hand. The shape of this hand indicates sensitivity and creativity. It is an average-sized hand, which narrows towards the fingers, and the fingers themselves are also wider at the base and narr-ower towards the fingertips. The nails are long.

People with this type of hand have an artistic and original nature, and are often gifted with ESP, and in particular, prophetic dreams and the ability to hear hidden voices.

When the hand is stable, it means that the person is decisive, ambitious and success-oriented, particularly in the areas of painting, sculpture, music, writing and acting.

When the hand is softer and fuller, it is a sign that the person enjoys luxuries, and tends not to be achievement-oriented.

These people are pleas-ant, impulsive and quite gene-rous, and hate prejudice, lies and deception. They are clever, quick-thinking and brilliant in social situations.

THE SPIRITUAL HAND

This is the rarest type of hand. The palm is narrow and the fingers are thin and conical. The nails are long and the general impression is that of tenderness and fragility. People with this type of hand are gentle and have a good heart; they love to help those who are suffering and are needy, and pour out their love to every living creature.

They are not ambitious. A rough and materialistic environment is likely to hurt them easily. This type of person usually has the ability to understand universal truths, and they are ahead of their time regarding spiritual development.

They are beautiful people, generally speaking, and have very expressive eyes. Occasionally they live their lives in loneliness, because it is hard for them to put their inner experiences into words.

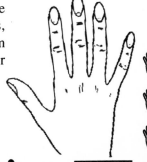

THE MIXED HAND

This is a hand that has the characteristics of several different types of hands. People with this kind of hand are usually multifaceted, unpredictable and restless. They often change their jobs and their ideas, and they quickly adapt to new people and situations. They hate routine and need constant stimulation.

It is hard for these people to complete a plan or a task, despite the fact that they are usually intelligent and original. They possess personal charm, are witty conversationalists, and have a talent for influencing others.

CHIROMANCY

Now that we have studied the shape of the hand and the fingers, and have learned how to obtain a general impression, we can go on to learn about the details of the palm: the mounts, the lines and other distinguishing marks.

THE MOUNTS

5 Mount of Venus
7 Mount of Mars
1 Mount of Jupiter
2 Mount of Saturn
3 Mount of the Sun (Apollo)
4 Mount of Mercury
8 Rectangle of Mars
6 Lunar Mount

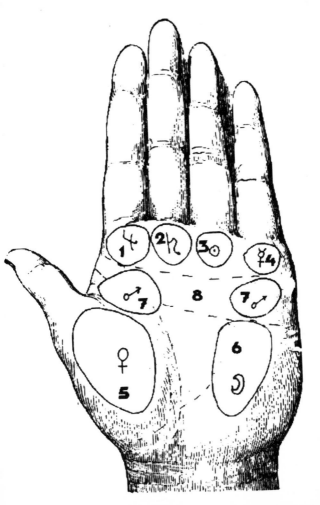

THE LINES

1 Life Line
2 Head Line
3 Heart Line
4 Fate Line
5 Sun Line
6 Health Line
7 Intuition Line
8 Girdle of Venus
9 Marriage Line
10 Lines of Children
11 Three Bracelets

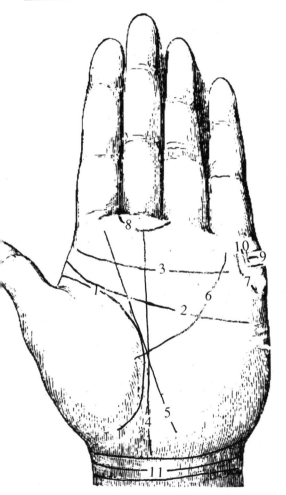

MARKS FOUND
ON THE PALM

Dot   . • .

Cross   + ×

Star   * *

Circle   O •

Island   ─o─

Square   ♯

Angle   ∧ ⌒ ∠

Triangle △ ▽

Grill (Grid)   ⌗

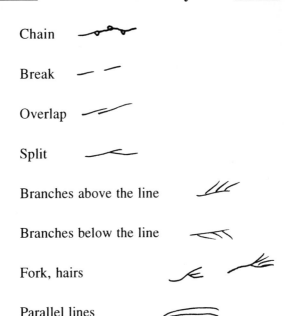

Chain

Break

Overlap

Split

Branches above the line

Branches below the line

Fork, hairs

Parallel lines

The five major marks will be described later in the text.

THE MOUNTS

These refer to the different areas on the palm of the hand. The more developed a particular area is on the palm, the more obvious the character trait it represents.

THE MOUNT OF VENUS

The Mount of Venus is located at the base of the thumb. A prominent Mount of Venus signifies good health, strong character and sexual attraction. A flattened Mount of Venus signifies physical weakness. Lines on the Mount of Venus that branch off from the Life Line toward the thumb signify artistic abilities.

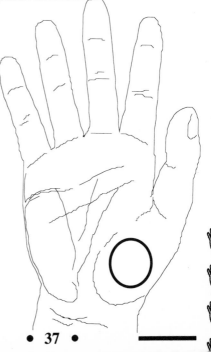

THE MOUNT OF THE MOON

Parallel to the Mount of Venus and below the Head Line, is the Mount of the Moon, or the Lunar Mount. A developed Lunar Mount indicates imagination, intelligence and fragility. When it is particularly developed, it means that the person is prone to fantasy. A flat Lunar Mount indicates an idealistic person, intelligent but not especially creative.

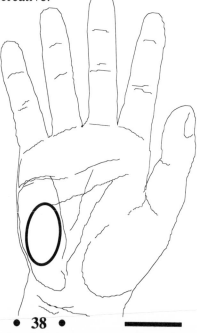

THE MOUNT OF MERCURY

The Mount of Mercury is located at the base of the pinkie. If this mount is average in size, it indicates a sense of humor and outstanding verbal ability. If the Mount of Mercury is flat, this means the person thinks slowly. When the mount is very broad, this shows a tendency towards deception and lying. A strong Head Line reinforces the positive traits of this mount. A weak Head Line stresses the negative traits.

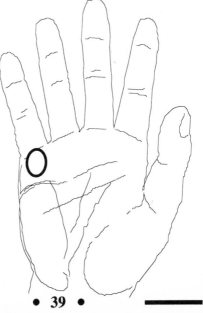

THE MOUNT OF THE SUN (APOLLO)

The Mount of the Sun is located at the base of the third finger near the pinkie. A moderate-sized mount indicates good luck, optimism and artistic abilities. A flattened mount means a lack of imagination, an indifference to the arts and no sense of humor. A particularly well-developed mount signifies a lack of self-discipline and a desire to be the center of attention. (This mount is also referred to as the Mount of Apollo.)

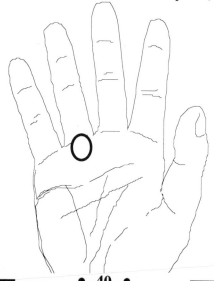

THE MOUNT OF SATURN

The Mount of Saturn is located at the base of the middle finger. If the mount is prominent, it indicates a tendency toward loneliness, a need for thought and deliberation, and a diligent and serious nature. As the mount becomes less prominent, this indicates that the person has a less serious approach to work and life.

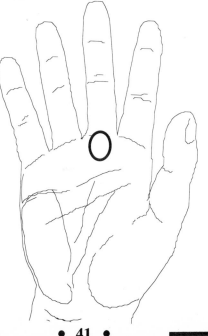

THE MOUNT OF JUPITER

The Mount of Jupiter is found at the base of the index finger. If the Mount of Jupiter is developed, it indicates ambition, enthusiasm, and self-confidence. A very prominent mount signifies that the person is conceited and domineering. A flat mount means sensitivity, but also a lack of insight.

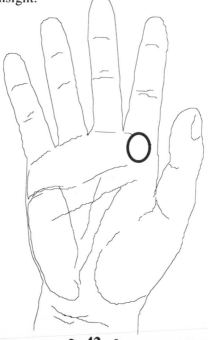

THE MOUNT OF MARS

There are two separate Mounts of Mars. The first Mount of Mars is located between the Mount of Mercury and the Mount of the Moon. If the mount is of average size, this indicates spiritual strength, self-control and balance. A very prominent mount indicates anger and a short temper. If the mount is small, it signifies an inability to face difficulties.

The second Mount of Mars is known as the Upper Mount of Mars, and is located between the Mount of Jupiter and the Mount of Venus. It signifies the person's physical strength, according to the size of the mount.

The two mounts are contained in a rectangle known as the Rectangle of Mars.

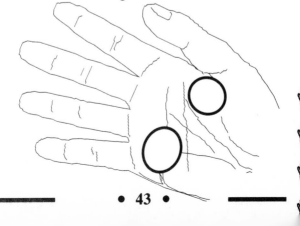

THE LINES OF THE HAND

The lines on the left hand reflect the basic characteristics of a person. The lines on the right hand indicate the development the person has undergone during the course of his life.

(For a left-handed person, the opposite is true.)

THE LIFE LINE

The Life Line begins beneath the Mount of Jupiter, goes around the Mount of Venus, and reaches the middle of the base of the hand. It teaches us about a person's vitality, strength and health. However, it does not foretell the length of a person's life or the circumstances of his death. A strong and clear Life Line indicates energy, willpower and good health in general. A short Life Line does not necessarily indicate a short life, but rather a lack of energy and power. Crosses that appear on the Life Line indicate periods of fatigue and a tendency toward mild illnesses. A break in the Life Line means a serious undermining of one's health. If the line continues after the break and resumes its course, this means that the person will regain his full strength. A line that begins at the Mount of Jupiter and not at the side of the palm signifies great ambition. A Life Line that begins together with the Head Line indicates intelligence and sensitivity. When there is a space that separates the two lines, this means a strong and aggressive personality. A very large space between the Life Line and the Head Line means that the person is impulsiveness and ignores his own wisdom.

Long

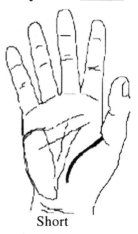

Short

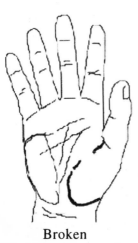

Broken

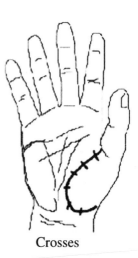

Crosses

THE HEAD LINE

The Head Line begins at the edge of the palm between the thumb and the index finger. It crosses the width of the hand in an almost horizontal line, and is related to intellectual skills and mental ability. If the Head Line is straight and clear, it indicates developed powers of thought and understanding, as well as an ability to concentrate. If the Head Line is short and weak, it usually signifies slow thinking and a tendency towards the practical rather than the abstract. When the Head Line starts together with the Life Line, it means that the person is overly smart, sensitive, or nervous; cautious and hesitant. The closer these two lines are to each other, and the more they are together, the more the person suffers from a lack of self-confidence. A small space between the Head Line and the Life Line indicates independence and originality. If the space between the two lines is too wide, it denotes selfishness, arrogance and a lack of caring. If the Head Line begins at the Mount of Mars, it shows that the person has a hot-tempered and volatile nature. If the Head Line proceeds downward towards the Mount of the Moon, it indicates imagination and artistic ability. If the line continues to the lower portion of the Lunar Mount, the person could be gifted with a great creative ability and unusual supernatural powers. If the Head Line tends towards the Mount of Mercury, it signifies mathematical and scientific abilities. A Head Line that tends towards the Mount of Apollo shows that the person utilizes his intellectual abilities for the purpose of accumulating money and wealth.

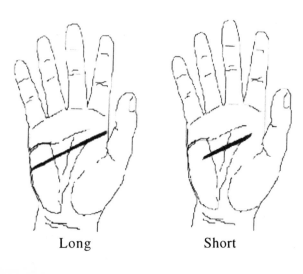

Long   Short

 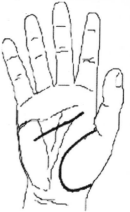

Close to the
Life Line

Far from the
Life Line

THE HEART LINE

The Heart Line can be found on the upper portion of the palm, at the base of the Mounts of Jupiter, Saturn, Apollo and Mercury. It reflects maturity and depth of feeling. If the Heart Line reaches all the way to the Mount of Jupiter, it indicates a balanced, warm and faithful personality. If the Heart Line splits between the Mounts of Jupiter and Saturn, it means the person has a personality that changes and is focused on himself. When the Heart Line begins underneath the Mount of Saturn, it shows that the person has shut off his emotions, and sometimes has difficulty expressing warmth and physical affection. Breaks in the line indicate disappointments in love. A low Heart Line, close to the Head Line, indicates that the person is controlled by his feelings, and they are clouding his judgment. A high Heart Line indicates just the opposite.

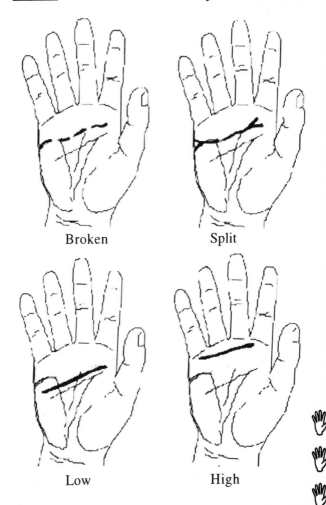

Broken   Split

Low   High

THE FATE LINE

The Fate Line is a vertical line in the center of the palm. It can begin at the base of the hand, the Mount of the Moon, the Mount of Venus, the Head Line, or sometimes even from the Heart Line. The Fate Line indicates success and failure in life. A Fate Line that begins at the base of the palm and continues straight along the hand to the Mount of Saturn signifies wealth and success. If the Fate Line begins with the Life Line, it means the person's childhood was spent in a restrictive environment in which he suffered from a lack of stimulation, encouragement and support. If the line continues clearly and strong, it means that the person has overcome the obstacles and has achieved objectives. When the Fate Line begins from the Mount of Venus, it indicates a great deal of help from loving people. A Fate Line beginning from the Lunar Mount denotes help from strangers, as well as a varied and fascinating life. If the Fate Line begins from the Head Line, it signifies self-fulfillment during the middle of the person's life. If the Fate Line begins at the Heart Line, this shows achievement following a difficult struggle later on in the person's life.

It is also important to note where the Fate Line ends: If it winds toward the direction of the Mount of Jupiter, the person is ambitious, decisive and intelligent, and will acquire status and power in the future. If the line ends at the Mount of Apollo or the Mount of Mercury, it indicates that errors in judgment are likely to ruin the person's chances for success. If the Fate Line ends at the Heart Line, this shows that emotions will become more important than striving for achievement.

A double Fate Line indicates success in two spheres. A break in the Fate Line indicates an obstacle. If there are chains on the Fate Line, this means a difficult period. A rectangle on the Fate Line means protection from an economic crisis. If a cross appears on the Fate Line, it signifies an accident or disaster.

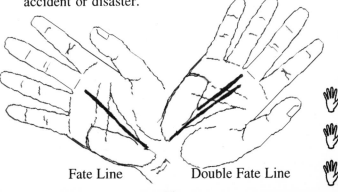

Fate Line   Double Fate Line

THE SUN LINE

The Sun Line (also known as the Line of Apollo) indicates fame and luck. This line is not always easy to find; it may begin from the Mount of the Moon or from the Life Line, the Head Line or the Heart Line, and continue toward the Mount of Apollo. If the Sun Line begins at the Lunar Mount, it indicates success, mainly because of the help and encouragement of others. If the Sun Line appears together with a diagonal Head Line, it denotes special artistic talent. If the Sun Line begins at the Life Line or the Heart Line, it signifies that the person has earned respect and property. When the Sun Line begins at the Head Line, this indicates great talent that will only acknowledged later on in life. If a star appears anywhere along the Sun Line, it means ongoing success. If a square appears on the Sun Line, it signifies protection from jealousy and the vindictiveness of others. If an island appears on the line, it indicates a temporary loss of status. A break or weakness in the line indicates obstacles and difficulties on the way to realizing one's ambitions. The lack of a visible Sun Line means the lack of goals and of confidence in one's personal abilities.

From the
Lunar Mount

From the
Life Line

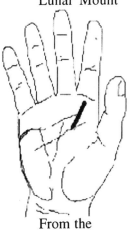

From the
Head Line

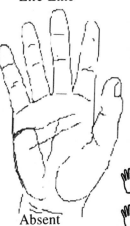

Absent
Sun Line

THE HEALTH LINE

The Health Line begins at the Mount of Mercury and descends along the length of the palm in the direction of the Mount of Venus. If the Health Line touches or crosses the Life Line, it signifies extreme vulnerability and a danger of illness and accidents. Small notches between the Health Line and the Life Line indicate headaches. Breaks along the Health Line may indicate stomach trouble. If the Health Line appears particularly red in color, it could mean heart-related problems. If the line is particularly pale, it indicates circulatory problems. A Health Line that is twisted and indistinct could indicate a tendency toward many minor illnesses. In general, the stronger the Health Line appears, the more impaired the person's health is. If the Health Line is missing completely, it signifies good health and physical strength.

Breaks

Indistinct Line

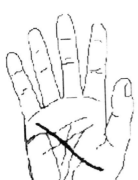

Crosses the
Life Line

Notches

THE INTUITION LINE

The Intuition Line begins at the Mount of Mercury and turns downward in a half-circle toward the Mount of the Moon at the base of the hand. If the Intuition Line is visible on both hands, this indicates sensitivity and well-developed ESP and awareness. If the Intuition Line is clearly defined on the left hand of a right-handed person (or vice versa for a left-handed person), this signifies that the person is greatly interested in the supernatural and is particularly open to ESP.

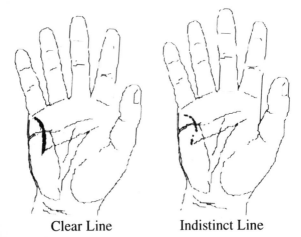

Clear Line   Indistinct Line

THE GIRDLE OF VENUS

The Girdle of Venus is a line shaped like a semi-circle, which begins at the index finger or the middle finger, and reaches the ring finger (next to the pinkie), or the pinkie. The Girdle of Venus indicates strong passions, though not necessarily of a sexual nature. The Girdle of Venus often signifies sensitivity and an especially sentimental personality, with extreme fluctuations of mood - a person who vacillates between enthusiasm and joy one minute and profound depression the next. If the Girdle of Venus is clear and unbroken, it shows a tendency toward hysteria and depression. If the Girdle of Venus ends up at the edge of the palm and touches the Line of Marriage, it means that the person is liable to spoil his relationships.

Clear Line

THE MARRIAGE LINES

The Marriage Lines are small lines located at the edge of the palm on the Mount of Mercury, and they can tell us about relationships. Long lines indicate marriage, while shorter lines inform us about love affairs or engagements. If the Marriage Lines are near the Heart Line, it indicates ease in finding a mate. When the Heart Line is near the center of the Mount, a mate will be found in the middle or towards the end of the person's twenties. If the Marriage Lines are found at the base of the pinkie, it shows that contact with the mate is expected after age thirty. If the line curves upwards, it signifies a possibility that the person will not marry at all.

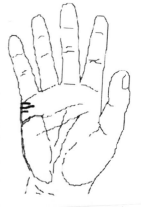

A strong Marriage Line without any breaks indicates a particularly good relationship. If the Marriage Line reaches the middle of the palm and then splits, it denotes a divorce. If the Marriage Line splits into two lines that reach the Mount of Apollo, it means the person's mate will be famous and successful.

THE LINES OF CHILDREN

Straight lines that continue from the edge of the Marriage Lines indicate children. Thicker, deeper lines signify boys, while weaker lines mean girls. If one of the lines is larger and more prominent than the others, it means that one of the children will be particularly talented.

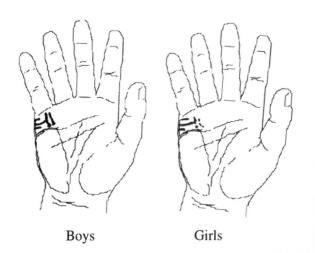

Boys   Girls

THE THREE BRACELETS

The Three Bracelets are three lines that go around the wrist. If the bracelets are strong and clear, this indicates good luck and good health. If the line closest to the hand is weak, the person will suffer from minor illnesses. If the line resembles a chain, it means great success following years of failure and disappointment.

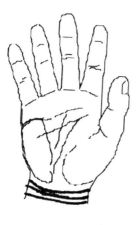

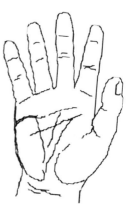

Strong bracelets   Weak bracelets

MARKS

The five principle marks are the Star, Cross, Triangle, Square and Island. These marks are of special significance, depending on the mount on which they are found.

Star

On the Mount of Venus - happiness and love.

On the Mount of the Moon - originality, imagination and intuition.

On the Mount of Jupiter - stubbornness, ambition and achievement.

On the Mount of Saturn - wisdom, imagination and a fatalistic attitude.

On the Mount of Apollo - artistic talents, fame, wealth and success.

On the Mount of Mercury - intellectual development and social status.

On the Lower Mount of Mars (beneath the Mount of Jupiter) - an ability to cope with the most trying situations successfully.

On the Upper Mount of Mars (above the Mount of Mercury) - great success following failure and difficulty.

Cross

On the Mount of Venus - family disputes.

On the Mount of the Moon - a tendency towards self-deception.

On the Mount of Jupiter - happy marriage.

On the Mount of Saturn - a fatalistic attitude and a weak character.

On the Mount of Apollo - disappointment.

On the Mount of Mercury - treacherous partners.

On the Lower Mount of Mars (beneath the Mount of Jupiter) - a dangerous situation and strife.

On the Upper Mount of Mars (above the Mount of Mercury) - jealous and disloyal friends.

Triangle

On the Mount of Venus - an intellectual approach.

On the Mount of the Moon - scientific, but also intuitive.

On the Mount of Jupiter - the ability to perform.

On the Mount of Saturn - imagination, intuition, and spiritual awareness.

On the Mount of Apollo - multifariousness, artistic talents, and success.

On the Mount of Mercury - personal charm and the ability to influence others.

On the Lower Mount of Mars (beneath the Mount of Jupiter) - quick and precise thinking.

On the Upper Mount of Mars (above the Mount of Mercury) - cool-headedness, self-control and logic.

Square

On the Mount of Venus - immunity from emotional difficulties.

On the Mount of the Moon - immunity from dangers while traveling.

On the Mount of Jupiter - proper appreciation of talents and opportunities.

On the Mount of Saturn - an optimistic approach towards life.

On the Mount of Apollo - a lack of interest in materialism.

On the Mount of Mercury - peace, immunity from stress and anxiety.

On the Lower Mount of Mars (beneath the Mount of Jupiter) - immunity from physical harm.

On the Upper Mount of Mars (above the Mount of Mercury) - immunity from acts of vengeance by enemies.

Island

On the Mount of Venus - frivolousness.

On the Mount of the Moon - melancholy.

On the Mount of Jupiter - inflated self-esteem.

On the Mount of Saturn - sickliness and depression.

On the Mount of Apollo - arrogance.

On the Mount of Mercury - a lack of peace and equilibrium.

On the Lower Mount of Mars (beneath the Mount of Jupiter) - a tendency toward excessive risk-taking.

On the Upper Mount of Mars (above the Mount of Mercury) - impulsive behavior.

DETERMINING AGE

We can use the lines on the palm to determine when a particular event will occur, or has already occurred. The age of the subject can be determined only by using the lines. If the particular event (indicated by a star, island, etc.) appears closer to the start of the line, we may assume it occurred at a younger age; and if the mark appears closer to the end of a line, we may assume that the event occurred at an older age.

From the cradle to the grave, the cycle of life is found on the palm.

There are two common methods for dividing the Life Line into ages.

1. Some divide a sample of the Life Line into sections that are equal in length, defining one end of the line as the first year of life, and the other as old age (traditionally 70). They then look at the different sections of the Life Line and determine what will occur, or what has occurred, in each one.

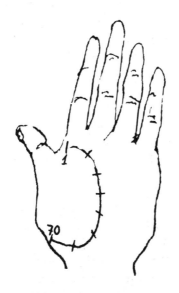

2. Another method for dividing the Life Line into ages is based on locating two points along the person's Life Line, one point representing 35 years old and the other point representing 49 years old.

These two numbers are related to 7 (5 x 7 and 7 x 7) since the number seven is very important in predicting the future. This method of dividing the Life Line is done in several steps:

A. Draw a line between the intersection point of the Head Line and the Fate Line, and between a point in the center of the Mount of Mercury (beneath the pinkie), and continue the line until it crosses the Life Line. This point represents age 35.

B. Draw a line from the lower end of the Head Line towards the center of the Mount of Venus. The point at which this line crosses the Life Line represents age 49.

C. Now divide the Life Line according to the ratio between the two points determined above. According to this method, the intersection of the Fate Line and the Head Line also represents 35 years of age on the Fate Line, and we may then divide the Fate Line into ages as well, with the earlier years of the subject's life being close to the wrist, and the later years being closer to the base of the fingers.

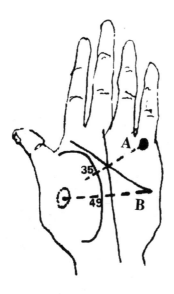